50 Premium Sandwiches for Every Taste

By: Kelly Johnson

Table of Contents

- Classic Lobster Roll
- Truffle Grilled Cheese
- Avocado and Bacon BLT
- Roasted Turkey with Cranberry and Brie
- Caprese Sandwich with Balsamic Glaze
- Pulled Pork and Coleslaw
- Grilled Chicken Caesar Wrap
- Spicy Tuna Melt
- Sweet and Spicy BBQ Chicken
- Grilled Portobello Mushroom and Pesto
- Smoked Salmon and Cream Cheese Bagel
- Beef Tenderloin with Horseradish Sauce
- Grilled Veggie and Hummus
- Cuban Sandwich
- Chicken Shawarma Wrap
- Roast Beef and Caramelized Onion
- Eggplant Parmesan Sub
- Spicy Chicken Banh Mi
- Tuna Salad with Pickles
- Pulled BBQ Jackfruit Sandwich
- Pesto Chicken and Mozzarella
- Shrimp Po' Boy
- Lobster and Avocado Sandwich
- Bacon, Lettuce, and Tomato with Fried Green Tomato
- Falafel with Tahini Sauce
- Grilled Cheese with Apple and Fig Jam
- Philly Cheesesteak
- Meatball Sub
- Duck Confit and Fig Jam Sandwich
- Chicken Schnitzel with Cabbage Slaw
- Grilled Tuna with Olive Tapenade
- Reuben with Swiss and Sauerkraut
- Roast Turkey and Avocado
- Pastrami and Swiss on Rye
- Sweet Potato and Black Bean Burger

- Teriyaki Chicken and Pineapple
- Steak and Cheese Sandwich
- Pork Schnitzel and Cabbage
- Roasted Chicken with Avocado and Chipotle Mayo
- Grilled Ham and Gruyère
- Brie, Pear, and Arugula Sandwich
- Mediterranean Veggie Wrap
- Spicy Italian Sausage and Peppers
- Thai Peanut Chicken Wrap
- Grilled Lamb and Tzatziki
- Smoked Turkey and Swiss with Honey Mustard
- Portobello Mushroom and Swiss
- Breakfast Sandwich with Bacon, Egg, and Avocado
- Grilled Cheese with Bacon and Tomato
- Smoked Brisket with Pickled Onions

Classic Lobster Roll

Ingredients:

- 1 lb cooked lobster meat, chopped
- 4 soft, buttery rolls (New England-style if possible)
- 1/4 cup mayonnaise
- 1 tablespoon lemon juice
- 1 tablespoon finely chopped celery
- 1 teaspoon Dijon mustard
- Salt and pepper, to taste
- Fresh parsley, for garnish

Instructions:

1. In a bowl, mix the chopped lobster meat, mayonnaise, lemon juice, celery, Dijon mustard, salt, and pepper.
2. Toast the rolls lightly until golden.
3. Spoon the lobster mixture generously into each roll.
4. Garnish with fresh parsley and serve immediately.

Truffle Grilled Cheese

Ingredients:

- 2 slices of sourdough bread
- 2 tablespoons truffle butter
- 1/2 cup grated Gruyère cheese
- 1/2 cup shredded mozzarella cheese
- 1 tablespoon truffle oil (optional for extra flavor)

Instructions:

1. Preheat a skillet over medium heat.
2. Spread the truffle butter on one side of each slice of bread.
3. Place one slice of bread butter-side-down in the skillet, add the Gruyère and mozzarella cheeses, and top with the second slice of bread, butter-side-up.
4. Grill until the bread is golden and the cheese is melted, flipping once to ensure both sides are evenly grilled.
5. Drizzle with truffle oil before serving, if desired.

Avocado and Bacon BLT

Ingredients:

- 2 slices of toasted whole wheat bread
- 2 slices of bacon
- 1/2 avocado, sliced
- 2 slices of tomato
- Lettuce leaves
- Mayonnaise

Instructions:

1. Cook the bacon until crispy.
2. Toast the bread slices.
3. Spread mayonnaise on one slice of bread.
4. Layer with lettuce, tomato, bacon, and avocado slices.
5. Top with the second slice of bread, cut in half, and serve.

Roasted Turkey with Cranberry and Brie

Ingredients:

- 2 slices of crusty bread
- 4 ounces sliced roasted turkey
- 2 slices Brie cheese
- 2 tablespoons cranberry sauce
- Fresh arugula

Instructions:

1. Layer the turkey slices on one slice of bread.
2. Top with Brie cheese and cranberry sauce.
3. Add fresh arugula for a bit of peppery crunch.
4. Close the sandwich with the second slice of bread, cut in half, and serve.

Caprese Sandwich with Balsamic Glaze

Ingredients:

- 2 slices of ciabatta or baguette
- 2 slices fresh mozzarella
- 2 slices ripe tomato
- Fresh basil leaves
- Balsamic glaze
- Olive oil

Instructions:

1. Drizzle olive oil on one slice of bread.
2. Layer with mozzarella, tomato slices, and fresh basil.
3. Drizzle with balsamic glaze.
4. Top with the second slice of bread and serve immediately.

Pulled Pork and Coleslaw

Ingredients:

- 2 slices of soft hamburger buns
- 1 cup pulled pork (pre-cooked or store-bought)
- 1/2 cup coleslaw
- Pickled jalapeños (optional)

Instructions:

1. Warm the pulled pork in a saucepan or microwave.
2. Toast the buns lightly.
3. Pile the pulled pork onto one bun and top with coleslaw.
4. Add pickled jalapeños for an extra kick, if desired.
5. Close the sandwich and serve.

Grilled Chicken Caesar Wrap

Ingredients:

- 1 whole wheat or spinach wrap
- 1 grilled chicken breast, sliced
- 2 tablespoons Caesar dressing
- Romaine lettuce, chopped
- Shredded Parmesan cheese
- Croutons (optional)

Instructions:

1. Lay the wrap flat and spread Caesar dressing in the center.
2. Layer the sliced grilled chicken, lettuce, Parmesan cheese, and croutons (if using).
3. Fold in the sides of the wrap and roll tightly.
4. Slice in half and serve.

Spicy Tuna Melt

Ingredients:

- 2 slices of sourdough bread
- 1 can of tuna, drained
- 1 tablespoon mayonnaise
- 1 teaspoon sriracha sauce
- 1 slice cheddar cheese
- Sliced jalapeños (optional)

Instructions:

1. In a bowl, mix the tuna with mayonnaise and sriracha sauce.
2. Toast the bread slices.
3. Spread the spicy tuna mixture on one slice of bread and top with a slice of cheddar cheese.
4. Add jalapeños for extra heat, if desired.
5. Grill the sandwich in a skillet until the cheese is melted and the bread is golden.
6. Serve hot.

Sweet and Spicy BBQ Chicken

Ingredients:

- 2 slices of toasted whole wheat bread
- 1 grilled chicken breast, sliced
- 2 tablespoons BBQ sauce (sweet and spicy variety)
- Sliced red onion
- Fresh cilantro

Instructions:

1. Coat the grilled chicken slices with BBQ sauce.
2. Toast the bread slices.
3. Layer the BBQ chicken on one slice of bread and top with red onion slices.
4. Garnish with fresh cilantro.
5. Close the sandwich, cut in half, and serve.

Grilled Portobello Mushroom and Pesto

Ingredients:

- 2 large Portobello mushrooms, cleaned and stems removed
- 2 slices of ciabatta or whole-grain bread
- 2 tablespoons pesto sauce
- Fresh mozzarella cheese, sliced
- Olive oil for grilling
- Fresh arugula or spinach (optional)

Instructions:

1. Preheat a grill or grill pan over medium heat.
2. Brush the Portobello mushrooms with olive oil and grill for about 4-5 minutes per side, until tender.
3. Toast the bread slices lightly on the grill.
4. Spread pesto sauce on one side of each slice of bread.
5. Place grilled mushrooms on one slice of bread, top with fresh mozzarella, and a handful of arugula or spinach.
6. Close the sandwich, cut in half, and serve.

Smoked Salmon and Cream Cheese Bagel

Ingredients:

- 1 bagel, halved
- 4 ounces smoked salmon
- 2 tablespoons cream cheese
- Sliced red onion
- Fresh dill for garnish
- Capers (optional)

Instructions:

1. Toast the bagel halves.
2. Spread cream cheese on the cut sides of the bagel.
3. Layer with smoked salmon, red onion slices, and capers if desired.
4. Garnish with fresh dill.
5. Close the bagel and enjoy!

Beef Tenderloin with Horseradish Sauce

Ingredients:

- 2 slices of baguette or a soft roll
- 6 oz beef tenderloin, cooked and sliced thinly
- 2 tablespoons horseradish sauce
- Arugula or watercress
- Salt and pepper to taste

Instructions:

1. Slice the beef tenderloin thinly.
2. Toast the bread slices lightly.
3. Spread horseradish sauce on one slice of the bread.
4. Layer the beef tenderloin slices, arugula, and season with salt and pepper.
5. Close the sandwich, cut, and serve.

Grilled Veggie and Hummus

Ingredients:

- 2 slices of whole wheat bread
- 1 zucchini, sliced
- 1 red bell pepper, sliced
- 1/2 eggplant, sliced
- 1 tablespoon olive oil
- 2 tablespoons hummus
- Fresh basil or arugula

Instructions:

1. Preheat a grill or grill pan over medium heat.
2. Toss the zucchini, bell pepper, and eggplant slices with olive oil and grill for about 3-4 minutes per side.
3. Toast the bread slices lightly.
4. Spread hummus on one slice of bread.
5. Layer with the grilled vegetables and fresh basil or arugula.
6. Close the sandwich and serve.

Cuban Sandwich

Ingredients:

- 1 Cuban roll or soft baguette
- 4 oz roast pork, sliced
- 2 oz ham, sliced
- 2 slices Swiss cheese
- 2 tablespoons yellow mustard
- 2-3 pickles, sliced

Instructions:

1. Preheat a sandwich press or skillet.
2. Spread mustard on both sides of the Cuban roll.
3. Layer the roast pork, ham, Swiss cheese, and pickles.
4. Press the sandwich in the pan or sandwich press until the bread is golden and the cheese is melted.
5. Slice and serve.

Chicken Shawarma Wrap

Ingredients:

- 1 large flour tortilla
- 1 grilled chicken breast, sliced
- 2 tablespoons tahini sauce
- 1/4 cucumber, thinly sliced
- Fresh parsley
- Romaine lettuce

Instructions:

1. Warm the flour tortilla in a skillet.
2. Spread tahini sauce on the tortilla.
3. Layer with grilled chicken, cucumber, parsley, and lettuce.
4. Roll up the tortilla tightly and serve.

Roast Beef and Caramelized Onion

Ingredients:

- 2 slices of rye bread
- 4 oz roast beef, sliced
- 1/2 onion, thinly sliced
- 1 tablespoon olive oil
- 1 tablespoon balsamic vinegar
- Swiss cheese (optional)

Instructions:

1. Heat olive oil in a skillet over medium heat, and sauté the onions until golden brown, about 8 minutes. Add balsamic vinegar and cook for another minute.
2. Toast the rye bread slices.
3. Layer the roast beef, caramelized onions, and Swiss cheese (if using) on one slice of bread.
4. Top with the other slice of bread, cut, and serve.

Eggplant Parmesan Sub

Ingredients:

- 1 sub roll or baguette
- 1 eggplant, sliced into rounds
- 1/2 cup marinara sauce
- 1/2 cup mozzarella cheese
- Fresh basil leaves

Instructions:

1. Preheat the oven to 400°F (200°C).
2. Place eggplant slices on a baking sheet and bake for about 15 minutes, until tender.
3. Toast the sub roll in the oven for a few minutes.
4. Spread marinara sauce on the bottom of the sub roll, add eggplant slices, top with mozzarella cheese, and bake until the cheese melts.
5. Garnish with fresh basil and serve.

Spicy Chicken Banh Mi

Ingredients:

- 1 baguette
- 1 grilled chicken breast, sliced
- 1/4 cup pickled carrots and daikon radish
- 1 jalapeño, sliced
- Fresh cilantro
- Mayonnaise
- Soy sauce (optional)

Instructions:

1. Slice the baguette and lightly toast it.
2. Spread mayonnaise on one side of the bread.
3. Layer with grilled chicken, pickled carrots, daikon radish, jalapeños, and fresh cilantro.
4. Drizzle with a little soy sauce if desired.
5. Close the sandwich and serve.

Tuna Salad with Pickles

Ingredients:

- 2 slices of whole-grain bread
- 1 can of tuna, drained
- 2 tablespoons mayonnaise
- 1 tablespoon Dijon mustard
- 1-2 pickles, sliced
- Fresh lettuce

Instructions:

1. In a bowl, mix the tuna, mayonnaise, and Dijon mustard.
2. Toast the bread slices.
3. Spread the tuna salad on one slice of bread.
4. Top with pickles and lettuce.
5. Close the sandwich and serve.

Pulled BBQ Jackfruit Sandwich

Ingredients:

- 1 can young green jackfruit, drained and shredded
- 1/2 cup BBQ sauce
- 2 sandwich rolls
- Pickled red onions
- Fresh cilantro

Instructions:

1. Heat a pan over medium heat and sauté the shredded jackfruit for 5-7 minutes.
2. Add BBQ sauce and cook for another 3-4 minutes, stirring to coat the jackfruit.
3. Toast the sandwich rolls lightly.
4. Layer the pulled BBQ jackfruit on the rolls and top with pickled red onions and fresh cilantro.
5. Close the sandwich and serve.

Pesto Chicken and Mozzarella

Ingredients:

- 2 slices of ciabatta or French bread
- 1 grilled chicken breast, sliced
- 2 tablespoons pesto sauce
- Fresh mozzarella cheese, sliced
- Arugula or spinach

Instructions:

1. Toast the bread slices lightly.
2. Spread pesto sauce on both slices of bread.
3. Layer with grilled chicken slices, fresh mozzarella, and arugula or spinach.
4. Close the sandwich, cut in half, and serve.

Shrimp Po' Boy

Ingredients:

- 2 soft baguette rolls
- 6-8 large shrimp, peeled and deveined
- 1/2 cup flour
- 1/4 teaspoon cayenne pepper
- 1/4 teaspoon paprika
- Lettuce
- Tomato slices
- Remoulade sauce

Instructions:

1. Mix flour, cayenne, and paprika in a bowl, and dredge the shrimp in the flour mixture.
2. Fry the shrimp in hot oil until golden and crispy, about 2-3 minutes per side.
3. Toast the baguette rolls.
4. Spread remoulade sauce on the rolls, then layer with lettuce, tomato, and fried shrimp.
5. Close the sandwich and serve.

Lobster and Avocado Sandwich

Ingredients:

- 2 slices of toasted brioche or soft roll
- 1/2 cup lobster meat, cooked and chopped
- 1/2 avocado, sliced
- Lemon aioli (or mayonnaise with lemon juice)
- Fresh herbs (parsley or tarragon)

Instructions:

1. Toast the bread slices.
2. Spread lemon aioli on one side of the bread.
3. Layer with lobster meat, avocado slices, and fresh herbs.
4. Close the sandwich, cut in half, and serve.

Bacon, Lettuce, and Tomato with Fried Green Tomato

Ingredients:

- 2 slices of toasted white or whole wheat bread
- 2 slices fried green tomatoes
- 2-3 slices crispy bacon
- Lettuce
- Tomato slices
- Mayonnaise

Instructions:

1. Toast the bread slices.
2. Spread mayonnaise on both sides of the bread.
3. Layer with fried green tomatoes, crispy bacon, fresh lettuce, and tomato slices.
4. Close the sandwich, cut in half, and serve.

Falafel with Tahini Sauce

Ingredients:

- 1 pita bread or flatbread
- 3-4 falafel balls, cooked
- 1/4 cup tahini sauce
- Fresh cucumber, tomato, and red onion slices
- Fresh parsley

Instructions:

1. Warm the pita bread.
2. Cut the falafel into halves or leave them whole.
3. Spread tahini sauce on the pita.
4. Layer with falafel, cucumber, tomato, red onion, and fresh parsley.
5. Close the pita and serve.

Grilled Cheese with Apple and Fig Jam

Ingredients:

- 2 slices of sourdough or whole-grain bread
- 2 slices sharp cheddar cheese
- 1/2 apple, thinly sliced
- 1 tablespoon fig jam
- Butter for grilling

Instructions:

1. Butter the outside of both slices of bread.
2. Spread fig jam on the inside of one slice of bread.
3. Layer with cheese slices and apple slices.
4. Close the sandwich and grill in a pan over medium heat for 3-4 minutes per side until golden and the cheese melts.
5. Cut in half and serve.

Philly Cheesesteak

Ingredients:

- 1 hoagie roll
- 6 oz thinly sliced rib-eye steak
- 1/4 onion, thinly sliced
- 1/4 bell pepper, sliced
- 2 slices provolone cheese
- Olive oil for sautéing

Instructions:

1. Sauté the onions and bell peppers in olive oil until soft, about 5 minutes.
2. Add the sliced steak to the pan and cook until browned, about 5 minutes.
3. Toast the hoagie roll.
4. Layer the steak mixture on the roll, top with provolone cheese, and melt the cheese under a broiler for a minute if desired.
5. Close the sandwich and serve.

Meatball Sub

Ingredients:

- 1 sub roll
- 4-5 meatballs, cooked
- 1/2 cup marinara sauce
- 2 slices mozzarella cheese
- Fresh basil leaves

Instructions:

1. Heat the marinara sauce and meatballs in a pan for a few minutes.
2. Toast the sub roll.
3. Place meatballs in the roll, cover with marinara sauce, and top with mozzarella cheese.
4. Melt the cheese under the broiler if desired, then garnish with fresh basil.
5. Close the sandwich and serve.

Duck Confit and Fig Jam Sandwich

Ingredients:

- 2 slices of baguette or soft roll
- 1/2 cup duck confit, shredded
- 1 tablespoon fig jam
- Fresh arugula
- Sliced brie cheese (optional)

Instructions:

1. Warm the duck confit in a skillet.
2. Toast the bread slices lightly.
3. Spread fig jam on one side of each slice of bread.
4. Layer the shredded duck confit, fresh arugula, and brie cheese (if using) on the bread.
5. Close the sandwich and serve.

Chicken Schnitzel with Cabbage Slaw

Ingredients:

- 2 slices of toasted white or whole wheat bread
- 1 crispy chicken schnitzel
- 1/2 cup cabbage slaw (shredded cabbage, carrots, and mayo or vinegar dressing)
- Dijon mustard (optional)

Instructions:

1. Toast the bread slices.
2. Place the crispy chicken schnitzel on one slice of bread.
3. Top with a generous serving of cabbage slaw.
4. Spread Dijon mustard on the other slice of bread (optional).
5. Close the sandwich and serve.

Grilled Tuna with Olive Tapenade

Ingredients:

- 2 slices of ciabatta or sourdough bread
- 1 can of tuna, drained
- 2 tablespoons olive tapenade
- Fresh lettuce
- Tomato slices

Instructions:

1. Grill or toast the bread slices lightly.
2. Mix the tuna with olive tapenade.
3. Layer fresh lettuce and tomato slices on one slice of bread.
4. Spread the tuna mixture on the other slice of bread.
5. Close the sandwich, cut in half, and serve.

Reuben with Swiss and Sauerkraut

Ingredients:

- 2 slices of rye bread
- 4-5 slices of corned beef
- 2 slices Swiss cheese
- 1/4 cup sauerkraut
- Russian dressing or Thousand Island dressing

Instructions:

1. Toast the rye bread slices.
2. Layer corned beef, Swiss cheese, and sauerkraut on one slice of bread.
3. Spread Russian dressing or Thousand Island dressing on the other slice.
4. Grill the sandwich on a skillet over medium heat until the cheese melts and the bread is crispy.
5. Serve hot and enjoy!

Roast Turkey and Avocado

Ingredients:

- 2 slices of whole-grain or sourdough bread
- 4-5 slices of roasted turkey breast
- 1/2 avocado, sliced
- Lettuce
- Tomato slices
- Mayonnaise or mustard

Instructions:

1. Toast the bread slices.
2. Spread mayonnaise or mustard on one slice of bread.
3. Layer with turkey slices, avocado, lettuce, and tomato on the bread.
4. Close the sandwich, cut in half, and serve.

Pastrami and Swiss on Rye

Ingredients:

- 2 slices of rye bread
- 4-5 slices pastrami
- 2 slices Swiss cheese
- Yellow mustard (optional)

Instructions:

1. Toast the rye bread slices.
2. Layer pastrami and Swiss cheese on one slice of bread.
3. Spread yellow mustard on the other slice of bread (optional).
4. Grill the sandwich on a skillet until the cheese melts and the bread is crispy.
5. Serve hot and enjoy!

Sweet Potato and Black Bean Burger

Ingredients:

- 2 sandwich rolls or buns
- 1 sweet potato, roasted and mashed
- 1/2 cup black beans, mashed
- 1 tablespoon breadcrumbs (optional)
- Lettuce
- Tomato slices
- Avocado slices
- Chipotle mayo or regular mayo

Instructions:

1. Mash the roasted sweet potato and black beans together with breadcrumbs.
2. Form into a patty and grill or pan-fry until crispy.
3. Toast the sandwich rolls or buns.
4. Spread chipotle mayo or regular mayo on both sides of the roll.
5. Layer the sweet potato and black bean burger with lettuce, tomato, and avocado.
6. Serve hot.

Teriyaki Chicken and Pineapple

Ingredients:

- 2 slices of toasted burger buns or soft rolls
- 1 grilled chicken breast
- 2-3 slices of fresh pineapple
- Teriyaki sauce
- Lettuce or arugula

Instructions:

1. Grill or pan-fry the chicken breast and brush with teriyaki sauce.
2. Toast the sandwich buns or rolls.
3. Layer the teriyaki chicken and fresh pineapple slices on the bottom bun.
4. Add lettuce or arugula on top.
5. Close the sandwich, cut in half, and serve.

Steak and Cheese Sandwich

Ingredients:

- 1 baguette or hoagie roll
- 6 oz rib-eye steak, thinly sliced
- 2 slices provolone or cheddar cheese
- Caramelized onions (optional)
- Fresh lettuce

Instructions:

1. Cook the steak slices in a pan until desired doneness.
2. Toast the baguette or hoagie roll.
3. Layer the steak, cheese slices, and caramelized onions (if using) on the bread.
4. Melt the cheese under the broiler or with a lid on the pan.
5. Add fresh lettuce, close the sandwich, and serve.

Pork Schnitzel and Cabbage

Ingredients:

- 2 slices of bread (preferably rye or whole grain)
- 1 crispy pork schnitzel
- 1/2 cup cabbage slaw (shredded cabbage, carrots, and vinegar dressing)
- Dijon mustard (optional)

Instructions:

1. Toast the bread slices.
2. Place the crispy pork schnitzel on one slice of bread.
3. Top with a generous amount of cabbage slaw.
4. Spread Dijon mustard on the other slice of bread (optional).
5. Close the sandwich and serve.

Roasted Chicken with Avocado and Chipotle Mayo

Ingredients:

- 2 slices of whole wheat or sourdough bread
- 1 roasted chicken breast, sliced
- 1/2 avocado, sliced
- Chipotle mayo (or regular mayo with a dash of chipotle powder)
- Lettuce

Instructions:

1. Toast the bread slices.
2. Spread chipotle mayo on one slice of bread.
3. Layer the roasted chicken, avocado slices, and fresh lettuce.
4. Close the sandwich, cut in half, and serve.

Grilled Ham and Gruyère

Ingredients:

- 2 slices of sourdough or rustic bread
- 4-5 slices of ham (preferably smoked or honey-baked)
- 2 slices Gruyère cheese
- Dijon mustard (optional)
- Butter for grilling

Instructions:

1. Spread Dijon mustard (optional) on one side of each slice of bread.
2. Layer the ham and Gruyère cheese between the slices of bread.
3. Heat a skillet or grill pan over medium heat.
4. Butter the outside of the bread and grill the sandwich until golden brown and the cheese is melted, about 4-5 minutes per side.
5. Serve hot and enjoy!

Brie, Pear, and Arugula Sandwich

Ingredients:

- 2 slices of baguette or country bread
- 4-5 slices of Brie cheese
- 1 pear, thinly sliced
- A handful of arugula
- Honey (optional)

Instructions:

1. Layer the Brie slices on one slice of bread.
2. Add the thinly sliced pear and a handful of fresh arugula on top of the Brie.
3. Drizzle with a bit of honey if desired for a sweet touch.
4. Top with the second slice of bread.
5. Serve as is or grill lightly for a warm sandwich.

Mediterranean Veggie Wrap

Ingredients:

- 1 large whole-wheat wrap or pita
- 1/2 cup hummus
- 1/4 cup roasted red peppers, sliced
- 1/4 cup cucumber, thinly sliced
- 1/4 cup Kalamata olives, pitted and sliced
- 1/4 cup feta cheese, crumbled
- A handful of spinach or mixed greens

Instructions:

1. Spread a generous layer of hummus over the wrap.
2. Arrange the roasted red peppers, cucumber, olives, feta cheese, and spinach on top of the hummus.
3. Roll up the wrap tightly and slice in half to serve.

Spicy Italian Sausage and Peppers

Ingredients:

- 2 hoagie rolls or sub buns
- 2 spicy Italian sausages, cooked and sliced
- 1 bell pepper, sliced
- 1/2 onion, sliced
- Olive oil for sautéing
- Marinara sauce (optional)
- Provolone cheese (optional)

Instructions:

1. Heat olive oil in a skillet over medium heat and sauté the bell pepper and onion until tender, about 5-7 minutes.
2. Add the cooked sausage slices to the pan and heat through.
3. Optional: Spoon some marinara sauce over the sausage and veggies.
4. Toast the hoagie rolls, then layer with the sausage, peppers, onions, and provolone cheese (if using).
5. Serve hot and enjoy!

Thai Peanut Chicken Wrap

Ingredients:

- 1 large flour tortilla
- 1 grilled chicken breast, sliced
- 2 tablespoons peanut butter
- 1 tablespoon soy sauce
- 1 tablespoon honey
- 1 tablespoon rice vinegar
- 1/4 cup shredded carrots
- 1/4 cup chopped cucumber
- A handful of cilantro leaves

Instructions:

1. In a small bowl, whisk together the peanut butter, soy sauce, honey, and rice vinegar to make the peanut sauce.
2. Spread a thin layer of the peanut sauce on the tortilla.
3. Add the grilled chicken, shredded carrots, cucumber, and cilantro on top.
4. Roll up the tortilla tightly and slice in half to serve.

Grilled Lamb and Tzatziki

Ingredients:

- 2 slices of pita bread or a wrap
- 1/2 lb grilled lamb, thinly sliced
- 1/4 cup tzatziki sauce
- 1/4 cup cucumber, thinly sliced
- A handful of fresh mint or parsley

Instructions:

1. Warm the pita or wrap.
2. Layer the grilled lamb slices on the pita bread.
3. Drizzle tzatziki sauce over the lamb, and add the cucumber slices and fresh mint or parsley.
4. Roll the pita or wrap and serve immediately.

Smoked Turkey and Swiss with Honey Mustard

Ingredients:

- 2 slices of whole-grain or sourdough bread
- 4-5 slices smoked turkey
- 2 slices Swiss cheese
- 1 tablespoon honey mustard
- Lettuce or spinach (optional)
- Butter for grilling

Instructions:

1. Spread honey mustard on one side of each slice of bread.
2. Layer the smoked turkey and Swiss cheese between the slices of bread.
3. Heat a skillet over medium heat and butter the outside of the bread.
4. Grill the sandwich until golden brown and the cheese is melted, about 4-5 minutes per side.
5. Optionally, add lettuce or spinach before serving. Enjoy!

Portobello Mushroom and Swiss

Ingredients:

- 2 slices of whole-grain or rustic bread
- 2 large Portobello mushrooms, stems removed and sliced
- 2 slices Swiss cheese
- 1 tablespoon olive oil
- Salt and pepper to taste
- Butter for grilling

Instructions:

1. Heat olive oil in a skillet over medium heat.
2. Add the Portobello mushroom slices and cook until tender, about 5-7 minutes. Season with salt and pepper.
3. Place the Swiss cheese on top of the mushrooms during the last minute of cooking to melt.
4. Butter the outside of the bread and grill the sandwich in a skillet until golden brown, about 3-4 minutes per side.
5. Serve hot and enjoy!

Breakfast Sandwich with Bacon, Egg, and Avocado

Ingredients:

- 1 English muffin, split in half
- 2 slices cooked bacon
- 1 egg, cooked to your preference (fried, scrambled, etc.)
- 1/4 avocado, sliced
- Salt and pepper to taste
- Butter for toasting the muffin

Instructions:

1. Toast the English muffin halves until golden brown.
2. While the muffin is toasting, cook the bacon and the egg.
3. Once toasted, spread a small amount of butter on the muffin halves.
4. On the bottom half, layer the bacon, cooked egg, and sliced avocado.
5. Season with salt and pepper, then top with the other muffin half.
6. Serve immediately for a delicious breakfast sandwich!

Grilled Cheese with Bacon and Tomato

Ingredients:

- 2 slices of white or whole-grain bread
- 2 slices cheddar cheese
- 2 slices cooked bacon
- 2-3 slices tomato
- Butter for grilling

Instructions:

1. Place the cheese, bacon, and tomato slices between the two slices of bread.
2. Butter the outside of the bread.
3. Grill the sandwich in a skillet over medium heat, pressing slightly, until golden brown and the cheese has melted, about 4-5 minutes per side.
4. Serve hot and enjoy the crispy, melty goodness!

Smoked Brisket with Pickled Onions

Ingredients:

- 2 slices of rye or sandwich bread
- 1/2 lb smoked brisket, sliced
- 1/4 cup pickled red onions
- 1 tablespoon mustard or barbecue sauce (optional)
- Pickles (optional)

Instructions:

1. Layer the smoked brisket slices on one piece of bread.
2. Add a generous amount of pickled onions on top.
3. Optionally, spread mustard or barbecue sauce on the other slice of bread.
4. Top with pickles if desired, then close the sandwich.
5. For an extra touch, grill the sandwich in a skillet until the bread is golden brown and the brisket is heated through.
6. Serve and enjoy the smoky, tangy flavors!